UNSHAKEABLE
RETIREMENT

UNSHAKEABLE RETIREMENT
A Retirement Game Plan for Living Your American Dream

Copyright © 2022 Dale L. Tondryk
ISBN: 978-1-956220-16-2

Expert Press
www.ExpertPress.net

This publication is designed to provide accurate and authoritative information regarding the subject matter contained within. It should be understood that the author and publisher are not engaged in rendering legal, accounting or other financial service through this medium. The author and publisher shall not be liable for your misuse of this material and shall have neither liability nor responsibility to anyone with respect to any loss or damage caused, or alleged to be caused, directly or indirectly by the information contained in this book. The author and/or publisher do not guarantee that anyone following these strategies, suggestions, tips, ideas, or techniques will become successful. If legal advice or other expert assistance is required, the services of a competent professional should be sought.

All rights reserved. No portion of this book may be reproduced mechanically, electronically, or by any other means, including photocopying, without the written permission of the author. It is illegal to copy the book, post it to a website, or distribute it by any other means without permission from the author.

Expert Press
2 Shepard Hills Court
Little Rock, AR 72223
www.ExpertPress.net

Editing by Michael Hume
Copyediting by Wendy Lukasiewicz
Proofreading by Lori Price
Text design and composition by Emily Fritz

UNSHAKEABLE RETIREMENT

A RETIREMENT GAME PLAN

FOR LIVING YOUR AMERICAN DREAM

DALE L. TONDRYK

CONTENTS

Introduction 1

1 - Visualizing a Win 11

2 - Meet the Coach 21

3 - Why Don't People Plan for Retirement? 29

4 - Ups and Downs 39

5 - Achieving Success Together 53

6 - Terrifyingly Exhilarating 61

7 - Three "Investment Worlds" 71

8 - Securing an Income 79

9 - Exit Cards 87

10 - Unshakeable Retirement 95

Conclusion 107

About the Author 111

I want to thank my grandfather, Michael Tondryk, for having the courage to move to the United States and pursue his American Dream.

I also want to thank my mom and dad for not handing everything to me, but for teaching me the life lesson that "money does not grow on trees," and for encouraging me to work my first job, a paper route, at age ten.

This book is also dedicated to my clients. Thank you for letting me be part of your American Dream.

Unshakeable Retirement would not be possible without the encouragement and support I'm grateful to have had from my wife Katherine, from my family, and from Melanie McCoy, my "right hand" at Tondryk Wealth Management.

INTRODUCTION

Do you believe there's still such a thing as the American Dream?

I do. I'm living my American Dream every day. And every day, I work with people who are crafting their own American Dreams and making those dreams real through hard work, ingenuity, courage, and a little luck. You have my word: You can do the same. If you want to live your own American Dream and enjoy retirement on your own terms, you can make that happen. It's like a game—and you can play that game to win.

However, as with any athlete or sports team, winning your American Dream (and your dream retirement) requires planning. That's why our focus at Tondryk Wealth Management is to help our friends and clients create a winning game plan that gives them the best possible chance to live their own American Dream into—and through—the golden years of retirement.

You may think you need millions of dollars to have a dream retirement. That just isn't so. It never ceases to amaze me how folks who have had modest careers and average incomes can win the retirement game and enjoy their personal American Dream for years to come.

Just like the teams who win the Super Bowl or the World Series, you have to add those magic ingredients I mentioned earlier: hard work, ingenuity, courage, and a little luck.

And a solid, winning retirement game plan.

* * *

If my grandpa were still around—and boy, don't I wish he was—he would probably say you already have the "luck" piece covered because you're blessed to live in the United States, the true land of opportunity.

I couldn't agree more.

In the early 1900s, Grandpa escaped the growing threats of communism and socialism in his home country of Poland, arriving by ocean liner onto American shores. I could tell you he arrived without a cent to his name, but that's not true. He had nine cents in his pocket.

The type of ship Dale's grandfather came to the states on. (Illustration courtesy of www.heritage-ships.com.)

Grandpa ended up in the Midwest, and after applying those key ingredients of hard work, ingenuity, courage, and a little luck, he found himself living his own American Dream as an independent farmer with a hundred acres and a beautiful river running through his spread. As a boy, I remember picking rocks out of one of Grandpa's fields so he could plow and plant.

He married a girl from his home country, and they had eleven kids, one of whom was my father. Although Grandpa did have the good fortune to see two of his brothers when they, too, had the courage to come to the land of opportunity and seek their own fortunes, he never saw his parents or anyone else in his family again. (Grandpa did see one more family member much later in life—another brother he had left behind in Poland visited him in the United States sixty-five years later.)

Maybe you've heard stories like this before. As incredible as Grandpa's story was, it wasn't uncommon in those days. You could say America was built by people like my grandfather, who fled oppression to find and create their own American Dreams. They didn't have very many of the benefits we enjoy today. Far from being able to craft a winning game plan for their retirement, most of those hard-working folks had to make it up as they went along, planning as best they could with whatever opportunities life presented them.

You've heard similar stories, but have you ever stopped to really imagine what that must have been like? Having the courage as a teenager to leave your family, never to see them again, to make whatever you could get out of a new life in a foreign land? To start from scratch in a place where you didn't know the language, let alone the rules, customs, and culture? I can't imagine doing that myself. Thanks to the hard work, ingenuity, courage, and luck of my immediate ancestors, I don't have to. Thanks to them, I have more than a leg up, and I enjoy many comforts and benefits due at least in part to what they were able to accomplish.

Dale's grandfather on horseback

Yes, if Grandpa was still here, he would say I have the luck part covered. He would probably think I was a fool if I didn't take full advantage of my opportunity to put together a winning game plan and enjoy my own American Dream in retirement.

* * *

I mentioned that my grandparents had eleven kids, and one of them happens to be my personal hero: my dad. He learned the value of hard work and courage from his own dad, and he showed us every day what it meant to build a true American Dream.

Dale with his dad after winning the championship game.

Our family grew up in Minnesota, where my father worked a tough job at a paper mill. He didn't stop working when the five o'clock whistle blew. For one thing, he worked a lot of overtime, eager to set money aside to take care of his family (thanks, Dad) and our future. Dad had other skills and talents, and he didn't let those go to waste. He could build just about anything. After work and on weekends, he built everything from houses to football field goalposts. You can still find some of the things he built if you happen to drive through a couple of little Minnesota towns.

Picture that. During the times my dad was building houses for us, he would come home around midnight on most nights, having gone to work *after work* on a house he was building. He fell into bed and then got up early to head back to work at the paper mill. While he's working on a house, he does this just about every day. Except Sundays, maybe, when he might have a clothesline pole to install for a neighbor.

In spite of all that, Dad was still very active in the family. He made it to all our sports games and important events, and he never let us forget the meaning of family.

It might be hard to imagine, but many of us have similar stories about our own family heroes, and we enjoy the chance to build American Dreams in large part because of what they did. Thanks to them, we don't have to do exactly the same things. To have our own American Dream in retirement, here in the twenty-first century, we still need to apply those key ingredients that start with hard work and includes creating a great game plan for retirement.

My mom and dad were my first clients. Dad could build anything, but he hadn't given much thought to building a retirement game plan to make sure he and

Mom would be well provided for in their golden years. I helped my folks put together such a plan, and I'm happy to say it was my first success story. It made me want to help as many people as possible to win their own American Dream retirements.

* * *

I'm Dale Tondryk, founder and president of Tondryk Wealth Management. I present a radio program here in the twin cities of Minnesota, and I help clients create winning game plans for their retirement. I work hard every day to live up to the promise and potential I inherited from my father and grandfather. You'll learn more about me and my firm as we go along, but more importantly, you'll learn about yourself, your potential, and your opportunity to win your own American Dream in retirement with the benefit of some solid game planning.

If you've been a listener of our radio show, *The Retirement Playbook*, or our podcasts by the same title, this book will help you fill in the blanks with information we don't always have time to address on the air. We'll start where you are today—where else?—and in chapter 1, we'll begin to visualize exactly what that American Dream looks like for you, specifically, in your golden years.

In chapter 2, you'll learn more about your "coach." We'll talk about how my own journey led to our unique approach to retirement game planning here at Tondryk Wealth Management, and you'll understand more about why we do things the way we do.

Do you ever wonder why more people don't have a winning game plan for retirement? In chapters 3 and 4, we'll explore some of the barriers people encounter and the inevitable ups and downs along the way to retirement.

We believe our unique approach to retirement game planning is highly effective, but it all starts with the proper attitude and mindset toward building that American Dream. As I said, this is a game you can win, and in chapters 5 and 6, we describe the positive, optimistic attitude we take toward game planning with our clients, and we explore the terrifyingly exhilarating feeling many people get when they approach those golden years.

Chapter 7 introduces you to the "three worlds" of investing, and chapter 8 talks about how you can nail down a secure retirement using some of the most fantastic tools available for retirement-aged investors today. Dad and Grandpa didn't have anything like these!

In chapter 9, we explore how you can play your winning hand of cards as you exit your career and enter your American Dream retirement. In chapter 10, we reinforce the inspiration that you can dream big, plan well, and retire confidently with an unshakeable foundation for many years to come.

It takes those special ingredients of hard work, ingenuity, courage, and a little luck to win the retirement game and to live the American Dream throughout your sunset years. It also takes a winning retirement game plan to achieve unshakeable retirement.

Turn the page, and let's get to work on your American Dream retirement.

1
VISUALIZING A WIN

Let's take a look into the future. Your future. We won't need a crystal ball. We'll take a little imagination and apply it to what we know about your situation today. At some point, you're going to retire from your working career. After that, what does your life look like in retirement?

How will you be spending your time? You know the old cliché about "running out the clock" in a rocking chair. That's not you, though, is it? Okay, maybe you'll take a break and rest in a comfortable chair from time to time—and maybe that chair will rock—but that's not the way you imagine spending all your time in retirement. I'll bet you're imagining a more active lifestyle in your golden years. You're exercising three or four times a week (maybe more) so you can keep up with the grandkids. You might have joined that country club you've been eyeing. You're playing golf or tennis or pickleball. You're spending time with friends and family, and you're even finding time to go on dates with that person you've been living with for several decades. You're busy! In fact, I can't tell you how often I've heard clients say they're busier in retirement than they've ever been.

Will you travel? One of the things people most look forward to in retirement is a chance to travel like they couldn't do when the alarm clock went off every Monday morning. How will your travel look in retirement? Will it be confined to short road trips to see the kids and grandkids, or will you be one of those couples who gets to board the plane first, not because you need extra time but because you're a couple of the airline's most cherished frequent flyers? Will you cruise the seven seas? See distant lands on far-off continents you've only read about or seen in movies? What interests you most about travel? The history? The cultures? The food? There's nothing wrong with weekends with the grandkids, but you already know all about the history, culture, and food at their house. During your golden years, you probably imagine travel that's a bit more adventurous.

Where will you be living? Far too many people fail to create a winning game plan for their retirement and end up living in a nursing home. That's not what you imagine, is it? When they close their eyes and dream of a bright future, nobody pictures life in a nursing home. You might consider an active retirement community if or when you decide to downsize, but even that kind of move will take some planning. Before that, will you stay in the home you love? Maybe forever?

Imagine making the improvements and adding the things you've always dreamed of to make your home the castle you've long envisioned. Or will you have a second vacation home or cabin somewhere, and the ability to visit as often as you like?

How will you get around? Speaking of visiting places, how will you get there? Years after retirement, you probably won't be driving that car that's sitting out in the driveway today. It might no longer be able to take you where you want to go. What will you replace it with? Will you and your spouse be able to drive newer, fancier (and more reliable) vehicles to get around to your fun retirement activities? Will your car(s) last as long as your eyes and reflexes and ability to safely drive will last? How about combining transportation with travel by owning a nice SUV or even an RV?

How will you help others? Everyone's different. There are as many American Dreams, and American Dream retirements, as there are Americans. One thing people imagine when they think of their golden years is being able to help others—to "give back." Whether it's helping newly married family members, or contributing to college education for younger relatives, or even tithing in a meaningful way to a church or charity, helping others is one of the most satisfying accomplishments of people who have had a winning game plan for their retirement.

How will you feel? We've all heard too many stories about folks who spent their retirements being sick or debilitated in some way. That kind of retirement doesn't often last very long. When you close your eyes and dream, that is surely not what you picture for your retirement. Having an active retirement lifestyle will certainly contribute to your vitality and longevity—those thrice weekly workouts will pay off—but even the most robust and active among us will tend to get sick more often as we get older. Will you dread going to the doctor, and dread even more getting the bill for medical services? Or will you have a game plan that makes health care something you don't have to constantly worry about? Will you be able to afford to make going to the doctor just one more thing you fold into your busy schedule, between rounds of golf and trips to the park with the grandkids?

The Winning Game Plan

At Tondryk Wealth Management, we derive great satisfaction from helping people create a true game plan to "win" their American Dream retirement.

There are folks out there nearing retirement age who haven't really given their retirement much thought. For those folks, imagining what retirement will be like without a solid game plan might be a scary proposition. It's the rocking chair. The leftovers eaten while babysitting the grandkids. Car repairs. Medical bills. Nursing home.

We love helping people change that vision and to truly be able to visualize a win in retirement. We love helping folks trade in the rocking chair for the country club. The sputtering clunker for the swanky SUV. The weeks of babysitting for weeks on cruise ships. The nursing home for the beach house or lakeside cabin. You might not have all these things, but again, everyone's different, and every American Dream retirement features some things over others. The key is finding your own passion for a wonderful retirement and creating a game plan that gets you what you value most.

There are people for whom international travel holds no great attraction. Maybe it's the jet lag or a simple distaste for flying. Those folks might greatly prefer to own their travel in the form of a big, shiny RV they can take anywhere in the country and live in mobile style. Some people look forward to a time when they don't have to live in—and maintain—a big home (let alone two homes). Membership in an active retirement community might be the answer for them, where the American Dream of retirement might seem like living at the country club all day, every day.

Not everyone has a big family and lots of grandchildren to keep them busy. Some people dream of downsizing to a lock-it-and-leave-it apartment and spending most of their golden years in other parts of the country, or even in other countries. Some will want to emphasize travel. Some will want to emphasize time with family. For many, retirement is the chance to contribute meaningful amounts of time, energy, and resources to the causes they most care about. Some want a little bit of everything. They have a long bucket list.

One thing is clear: You won't win your American Dream retirement, whatever it is, without a great game plan to get you to the goal line. There are forces at play that will oppose your dream retirement and that must be defeated with a winning game plan.

Your Opponents

Your opponents in the dream retirement game can be beaten, but they'll put up a fight. Here are a few of the foes who will stand between you and your American Dream retirement, just waiting to throw you for a loss:

- » **Loss of income.** Those paychecks you used to get aren't coming anymore once you retire. You'll have Social Security, of course, but for most people, that's not enough income to replace the new money they're no longer making.

- » **Taxes.** Anyone who's been keeping up with the social and political changes in our country will tell you to look out for rising taxes. The taxman is sure to be one of your retirement's main foes.

- » **Inflation.** Everything you buy, from airline tickets to eggs, will likely cost more in a year or two than they cost today. A winning retirement game plan takes this into account and doesn't force you to try to pay tomorrow's prices with today's dollars.

- » **Health care.** No matter what you might hear from a newscast or politician, you can count on higher medical costs in the future.

Taken together, these "opponents" mean you're going to need more money in retirement than you might have imagined. If you have a solid game plan, you'll have what you need to beat these foes and get the retirement you deserve. Too often, when people take the time to imagine their own retirement, all they see when they close their eyes are these formidable opponents. They worry about these things. Some worry constantly.

We love to point out that they can take some hardy "teammates" into the game against these foes, and with the right game plan for their specific circumstances (and priorities), they can beat these guys.

Victory!

Not everyone is positioned for an overwhelming blowout victory over their retirement opponents, but just about everyone can win the retirement that matches their priorities and dreams. Some folks are downright amazed at what they can accomplish for their retirement and how soon they can start living that dream.

I recently had a conversation with a fifty-eight-year-old client who has been a great saver throughout his adult life. He might have the first penny he ever made safely tucked away. "Ted," as I'll call him, was living on far less than he made, and he told me that he figured on working until he was sixty-five. "After all, isn't that when people retire?" Ted asked.

After a quick review of Ted's situation, I was able to give him some good news.

"Just taking a first look at your retirement game plan," I said, "you have everything you need to cover your expenses. From your Social Security to your pension to the annuity income payments we've set up for you, you'll have more than enough. In fact, we don't even have to touch your 401(k) or deferred compensation savings." I then had a question for him: "How much do you love your job?"

Ted thought about it, and he told me he wasn't really loving his job at all these days. "I'm lucky to be working from home right now," he said. "The company's getting a little, well, crazy."

That's when I was able to give Ted the really good news.

"You don't have to wait until you're sixty-five. If you wanted to, Ted, you could retire today."

I showed Ted how we could set up a guaranteed income for him and ensure that he will never run out of money. This plan would still leave him plenty of money to pass on to his kids or grandkids (or contribute in any way he chose).

Ted won! He spends his time with his grandkids now and does what he wants. No more "crazy" job to worry about.

Not everyone is positioned as well as Ted was for early retirement. Even so, with a winning game plan, you might be surprised how well you could do and how early you could stop working at *your* crazy job.

* * *

No matter what kind of American Dream retirement you envision, the one big question on most retirees' minds is this: Will we run out of money? Other questions follow from that. Will we have to spend our last years in that nursing home we don't even want to visit? Will we fail to fully enjoy our retirement and leave too much on the table? Will we watch the cruise ship sail out of our future from our vantage point in the rocking chair? Will we live in fear of poverty and leave it to our children to buy country club memberships with our hard-earned money?

Let's make a plan that keeps none of these things from happening.

Visualizing a win is important. Any pro athlete in just about any sport will tell you it's almost as important to visualize success as it is to execute the things you need to do to be successful. The pro golfer doesn't swing the club until she's visualized exactly where the ball will go and which flight path will take it there. The quarterback reads the defense and visualizes how the defenders will react to the play he's called. The big-league pitcher visualizes every pitch he makes.

At an early age, I realized the power of a good imagination to visualize a win. When you can envision your own victory, you can get to work making a winning game plan to get you there.

Let's meet the retirement coach who's going to help you create just such a plan.

2
MEET THE COACH

Many professional sports coaches—some would say the best coaches—started out as players. Your retirement coach (me) is no different.

As you can probably tell, I love sports. In my school days, I played football, among other things. I'll never forget the day I first began to realize the power of visualizing victory. We were little seventh graders, my buddies and me, and we were walking off the football field after a typical tough practice.

"Someday," I said, "we're going to win the state championship."

I think one or two of the guys might have laughed at my prediction. I think they also knew there was just something about this team that combined the elements of a championship. We could feel it. We had growing ability, of course, but it was more than that.

It was an attitude, a positive mental spirit that seemed to whisper to us that we couldn't help but become champions if we only kept working hard and listening to our coaches.

And believing.

Dale celebrates with his family after the championship game

As I said, I started to understand the power of visualization and positive attitude that day in seventh grade, but I didn't really realize how powerful it was until a few years later. Picture this: those same pals and I hoisting the state championship trophy we had won for our tiny little high school. Just as we had visualized. Just as we had predicted. Just as we had worked for and grown into and earned for ourselves, our community, and our families (all of whom were very proud of us). I can still vividly remember that championship season.

Winning the Retirement Game

I didn't end up coaching football, and sometimes I miss the game. I did become a successful coach of another sort, helping my mom and dad put together a winning game plan for their retirement, as I mentioned in the introduction.

The day I coached my parents toward a retirement plan that enabled them to live their golden years in the way they had always wanted, I was hooked. I wanted to share that feeling with as many people as I could. Of course, I wanted to win the retirement game myself, and I might as well have several Super Bowl trophies for the way I've played that game, but I also wanted to coach other hard-working folks to create the retirement that matched their own American Dreams.

Dale's parents, Marjorie and Lawrence Tondryk.

Retirement is a game you can win, if you have a solid and realistic game plan. Coaching people to create and execute those plans is my life's work. It's the reason, starting with the work I did for my parents, that I've always loved what I do. I have to say, there's nothing like the satisfaction of being able to give great news to people like Ted.

A Great Plan Starts with a Winning Philosophy

Our philosophy at Tondryk Wealth Management starts with the governing thought that retirement really is a game you can win. That's our starting point with every retirement game plan client. Whatever your circumstances at the time we meet you, we can help coach you to achieve your best possible retirement, based on your specific priorities.

It's not magic. It's just careful, thoughtful game planning that helps you start where you are and begin moving the ball in the direction of your best retirement.

There are seven main elements to our winning philosophy that help us create excellent retirement game plans for our clients. First, there is no crystal ball. I sure wish there were, but here's the simple truth: The equity markets upon which so many investors plan to rely on in retirement are *reactive*, which means they react to major events that happen randomly. No one can predict the future; therefore, no one can really predict what your portfolio is going to do when it's left to the ups and downs of what we call the "Wall Street casino." That's why a smart approach to retirement game planning is to move at least some of your assets into guaranteed instruments that will allow you modest growth without fear of losing the whole ball game.

Second, consistency is king. A great retirement game plan calls for choosing financial tools that allow for more consistent, if not dramatic, growth over time. There are portfolio managers (stockbrokers and salespeople) out there who will point to a 45 percent growth in a certain fund or equity this year and suggest you jump on it. They don't own the aforementioned crystal ball, so they don't know that your investment won't suffer a severe loss the next year. (In fact, investments that shoot up one year have a way of crumbling down the next. Talk about dramatic!) When you're young and playing blackjack at the casino, drama and excitement might be called for, especially if you can afford to lose your chips. In retirement, when you're not earning new money, you can't afford the theatrics. A consistent, safe portfolio is always better in retirement.

Third, tax planning is crucial. I've said it before, on my radio program, and elsewhere, that the seven most expensive words in the English language are "My CPA takes care of my taxes." Nothing against hard-working, sharp CPAs. However, in my experience, most of them operate more as "tax filers" than as "tax planners." Since the taxman is one of your biggest opponents—the burliest tackler waiting to sack your retirement, so to speak—tax planning is absolutely essential and is part of any great retirement game plan. For instance, we coach our clients on simple things, like converting a rollover IRA to a Roth IRA, to protect them from the taxman in retirement.

Fourth, your emotions can lose the game for you. Just like the outfielder who thinks he can throw a speedy runner out at the plate but instead allows two other runners to advance into scoring position, too many investors make quick, emotional decisions that can have severe consequences for their retirement nest egg. A big part of our coaching involves helping our clients understand that sticking to their plan is their best bet—though it isn't a bet at all. When you get free advice from a pal or neighbor that a certain stock is red hot, check with your coach first before you put your nest egg at risk. That pal or neighbor doesn't know any more about the future performance of that equity than anyone else. When you put your retirement funds at risk, you might well lose a lot of money that you won't have time to recover.

Fifth, nothing lasts forever, and that includes Social Security. Social Security has been around since a time few living people can remember, so many folks nearing or at retirement age have grown up with the notion that it's "forever." There are a few harsh facts we all need to keep in mind. More and more people are living longer and taking more and more money out of the Social Security till. Fewer and fewer dollars are being paid into the program to support it, since the population is aging and the younger generations have different ideas about careers and working from what their forebears had. Meanwhile, the whole program is subject to the federal government, which many people believe is not the most fiscally responsible entity on Earth. Put these all together, and change is inevitable.

Sixth, the Grim Reaper is undefeated. We're living longer in our society than folks did in our grandparents' generation, but nobody outplays the Reaper. One of my favorite quotes comes from Andy Rooney, who said, "The idea of living a long life appeals to everyone, but the idea of getting old doesn't appeal to anyone." So true. Before the Reaper finds us (sometimes long before), we may be unable to do the fun stuff we used to do, or we may be unable to care for ourselves on a daily basis. To be ready when that day comes, any great retirement game plan includes some kind of provision for long-term care.

Seventh, you don't win the game without good coaching. Take two people who want to lose weight and get in shape. One makes it up as he goes, subject to the same cravings and laziness that afflict us all; the other, possibly more dedicated, gets a nutrition counselor and personal trainer. Who do you think will have a better outcome in three, six, or twelve months? The same goes for retirement. When you have meaningful goals, and when you're serious about achieving those goals, you seek out expert help. Having an expert retirement coach gives you a much better chance of winning your American Dream retirement than trying to go it alone.

We'll explore each of these elements in greater detail as *Unshakeable Retirement* unfolds.

* * *

Given the great benefits of getting expert retirement coaching—learning you can retire better and earlier—you would think everyone would want a good retirement game plan and a strong coach to help them win. So what's stopping some folks from getting that fantastic leg up on the opponents we all face in retirement?

Let's explore that next.

3
WHY DON'T PEOPLE PLAN FOR RETIREMENT?

Suppose you owned a professional hockey franchise, and your approach was to accumulate the best players you could afford and then send them out onto the ice each evening with a stirring cry of "Go, fight, win!"

No game plan. No real "plays" to practice. No practice, for that matter!

And no coach.

You wouldn't take that approach, of course, because it would be ridiculous. You would know with that kind of approach, your team would be unlikely to win many games. Without some planning and some smart coaching, you're unlikely to win your American Dream retirement too.

Just the other day, I met with a nice couple nearing retirement who you might say had taken a similar approach to handling their golden years. They had accumulated some nice "players." They had sold their home and downsized to a paid-off townhouse, they owned a business they had been able to sell, and they had a fair amount of money in cash in the bank. They weren't nearly as foolish as the daft hockey owner described above—after all, they were in my office asking questions—but for a variety of reasons, they hadn't done any planning for their retirement. Their first quandary was to tell me they didn't have any idea what to do with that cash.

As always, my approach was to "start where you are." I asked how much they thought they would need in retirement. They threw out a number ($8,000 per month) that was twice the amount of their monthly Social Security payments and based on no real analysis.

"If you need that much every month," I said, "you'll run out of money."

They were shocked. The thought that they might run out of money had never occurred to them.

"Do you really need that much?" I quickly asked. "Your home's paid off, and you have no real expenses beyond the usual stuff, like utility bills and food."

I love working with folks like these. We were able to assemble their players into a cohesive, well-coached team. We made sure that all of their must-pay expenses could be paid from guaranteed income sources, and we showed them how they could enjoy a wonderful retirement on far less than $8,000 per month—without ever worrying about running out of money.

This couple hadn't done anything wrong. They had done a good job, in fact, getting the players assembled on their bench. They just needed a good, seasoned coach and a winning retirement game plan.

Some People Are Too Busy to Think about Retirement

They're too busy, until it's time to retire.

One of the biggest reasons people get to retirement time without a retirement plan is that life has simply been too busy to permit any sober thought about how their golden years would, or could, go. They've just been socking away money in a 401(k) plan, for instance, or thinking they would be able to rely on a pension or on Social Security payments, along with whatever cash they had been able to save during their hectic working years. Then one day they realize they have some hopes for their retirement years but no real clue about whether those hopes and dreams can be made real with the assets they have.

We all tend to be drawn to activities and endeavors that make us feel successful. The knowns, more than the unknowns. The stuff we deal with every day, more than the big looming project, which, frankly, can be scary. For many people, it's easy to tell themselves they're too busy putting food on the table today to worry about what they'll need years from now.

But worry they do. That's why I really enjoy working

with people who come to see me right around retirement time with some accumulated assets and no real plan. Sure, I could have done more for them earlier, but there's still so much I can do for them today. When a couple walks into my office with a cloud of doubt and worry hanging over their heads, I can't tell you how much I love seeing them walk out later with most, if not all, of that cloud blown away.

Uncertainty creates fear. Fear creates doubt. Doubt leads to worry, and worry leads to indecision and inaction. Realizing you've failed to act creates more fear, and this leads to a vicious cycle that drags some people down into a bad situation that could have been avoided with a little smart coaching and planning.

We're all busy. I fully understand the hectic busyness, fear, and worry that keep people locked in a pattern of dealing with a busy daily life. It's been my experience that people who have been too busy during their working years to do any retirement planning will have a busy retirement too. But what will they be busy with? If they eventually let the coach draw up a great retirement game plan for them, they'll be busy with grandkids and golf and travel. If not, well, maybe they'll just be busy working.

That's not what anyone envisions when they close their eyes and dream. It's certainly not my aspiration for the people I'm privileged to meet.

You Don't Know What You Don't Know

Another big reason some people don't plan for retirement is that they don't know how, or they don't know anything about the tools and products available today for retirement investment and income. Retirement planning is my business, so I'm constantly working to keep up with the latest investment products, tax planning strategies, and retirement income vehicles. But my clients? They're lucky if they even realize that there's a whole world of retirement tools out there that they could use some help figuring out. As a result, some people don't know what a little retirement planning can do for them. They don't realize what their possibilities really are.

Here's a little secret that might surprise you: There's a good chance you can retire better and sooner than you ever thought possible. In fact, it wouldn't shock me if some study showed that nine out of ten folks could retire earlier than they expected to.

It's easy to assume that you just need to accumulate a massive amount of money—like a million bucks—and then, if you were able to do that, you wouldn't need to do any planning. That's kind of like the hockey example mentioned at the beginning of the chapter. People come to our office with far less than a million dollars, but they're thrilled to realize that they don't need a huge sum of money saved up in order to retire the way they would like to retire.

If you're working hard at a job that you don't particularly love, and you were to find out that you could leave that job tomorrow (or next year) and enjoy the retirement you had always hoped for, wouldn't that be worth exploring?

That can't happen for everyone, though you might be surprised at what your specific possibilities might be.

Do-It-Yourself Might Do in Your Retirement

I have great admiration for supersmart people, but I've come across some people who might be too smart for their own good. It's not uncommon for someone who's made a living with their sharp mind to believe they can "figure it out" when it comes to retirement planning. They can make retirement a DIY (Do-It-Yourself) project.

Unfortunately, these are often the folks who end up losing a large chunk of what might have been a nice retirement nest egg because they followed their intellectual instincts when it came to things like the stock market or other types of investing. To illustrate, suppose you owned a hockey franchise, but since you had been a successful and highly paid brain surgeon or engineer, you decided you could figure it out when it came to coaching your own hockey club.

The net would be pelted with puck after puck! Just not your opponent's net.

Here's a small sample of some trouble even a smart person can get into when they go it alone. Take the case of a couple who has, say, $600,000 in cash and some other investments. They could put those funds into tax-deferred products that would enable them to realize modest growth without risk of loss, and they could give themselves a much lower reportable income. This might enable them to take advantage of much lower tax rates and premiums for Medicare than if they were to report a whopping annual income of something in the neighborhood of $150,000. That strategy would stretch their retirement nest egg much further and give them a great deal more peace of mind. Even a genius astronaut won't necessarily know the ins and outs of retirement planning, or about strategies like this, which are second nature to those of us who are professional retirement planners.

A brilliant lawyer wouldn't perform her own eye surgery, no matter how many difficult and thorny cases she had argued and won. An award-winning architect probably wouldn't try to rebuild his vintage car's engine. Even the smartest among us would be well-served to seek the help of an experienced, knowledgeable pro—someone like me—when it comes to retirement planning.

Overreliance on Legacy Tools

The world has changed, and today, we don't have the kind of retirement tools our parents and grandparents had. Of course, they didn't have the kind of things we have either. In some cases, I come across folks who think they can use the same tools their parents used to retire.

Few big companies these days offer a true pension

plan. Instead, today's workers and executives have 401(k) plans, which in most cases are tied to the stock market and do include some risk of loss. Social Security is still hanging around, but who knows how long that will last. Even if you get Social Security payments throughout your retirement, they aren't likely to be as large (in terms of percentage of your working income) as the payments your grandparents enjoyed.

Too many retirement-aged folks think they can rely on Social Security, pension payments, and modest IRA accounts to fund their retirement. Those tools can be helpful players on your retirement roster, but without a true retirement plan that takes advantage of the best tools available on the market today, you're likely to miss out.

The Taxman Will Take a Big Bite

Even if you have a million dollars in your retirement nest egg, you should know that you really only have about $750,000 once you pay your "partner," Uncle Sam. One of the biggest reasons people fail to plan for their retirement is that they've underestimated the impact taxes are going to have on their savings.

The government and its programs are expanding these days. Unemployment is a problem, and underemployment an even deeper problem, both of which combine to mean fewer taxpayers are paying taxes to support this growth. The bottom line? The taxman has to take bigger and bigger bites out of people who have resources, and that list is certainly not limited to millionaires and billionaires. That means higher and ever-increasing taxes for regular retirees like you and me.

One of the best tactics we can recommend for our clients is to move at least some of their retirement money into instruments that are taxed at lower rates or with which the taxes are deferred. A Roth IRA, for instance, is vastly superior to a regular IRA for most of our clients.

Again, folks who don't do much retirement planning or think they can go it alone, don't often know about some of the simplest moves they can make to protect and stretch their retirement funds.

* * *

Not long ago, a client visited our office who had been a facilities manager for a large company for many years. He hadn't had a highly compensated position, but he and his wife had been very good at managing their expenses and saving what they could throughout the man's working years. When I ran the numbers for them and told him he could retire anytime he wanted, the man turned to his wife and said, "Really?" It would be hard for me to forget this wonderful moment.

This hard-working man, who thought he would be maintaining buildings for a few more years, turned in his retirement notice the next day. Now, he and his wife enjoy their time doing whatever they want to do, day in and day out.

Not everyone can have a moment like this, and there are barriers to smooth retirement planning, which we'll explore next. It's amazing how often people come into our office and, with a little retirement game planning, realize they can retire better (and sooner) than they ever imagined.

4
UPS AND DOWNS

As in any sporting contest, the retirement game pits you against opponents who will try to defeat you and ruin your chance of winning your American Dream retirement. This analogy is a strong one because your retirement coach works on your behalf in much the same way a sports coach works on the team's behalf. Those opposing players? They can be defeated, and your retirement coach can help you do it.

Let's consider the case of a college volleyball team, and let's make it one with a strong winning tradition and a great, supersmart coach. How does that coach prepare the game plan for the next big match? She endlessly studies film to learn the tendencies of the coaches and players on the team she's about to face. She has her players watch the film too, and she points out weaknesses and vulnerabilities her team might exploit during the match. She also notes how the opposing team has taken advantage of their past opponents' weaknesses, and she studies the tendencies that may make her own team vulnerable to a particular strength on the other side.

"See how Number 11 tends to drift into the center after the first couple of volleys? She leaves her side of the court open. We need to be aware of that and look for it during the match. We can score some points on her side. See how good Number 19 is at disguising her best shots? We need to put a spy on her and not be fooled when she goes for the fake. If we can be ready for her tactics even half the time, we'll slow her team way down."

Stuff like that.

The winning volleyball coach studies her opponents' tendencies and comes up with a crafty plan for taking points off the board they might otherwise score, while at the same time putting points on the board for her own team that might not otherwise have been scored. Your retirement coach does essentially the same thing. A good retirement coach will have lots of experience working with retirees whose opponents scored against them, and with others who anticipated the opponents' tendencies, beat them to the ball, and achieved victory.

Even Biff Can't Predict the Market

In the movie *Back to the Future Part II* (which practically every American has seen at some point), the main antagonist, Biff, is able to steal our heroes' time machine and travel to the future, where he gets his hands on a sports almanac. He then goes back to his own time, and armed with certain knowledge of which teams will win the next several Super Bowls and World Series, he makes a fortune gambling on those events.

If I had such an almanac, I would quit the financial industry and become a full-time sports gambler. If I had a crystal ball, tea leaves, or a modern-day Nostradamus that could guarantee me certain knowledge of how specific stocks (or the market as a whole) would perform in the future, I would bet heavily in the Wall Street casino and never worry about losing money. I would make money hand over fist. Unfortunately, these precious tools aren't available. Not to me and not to you. Not to anyone. That's probably the reason even the smartest Wall Street investment advisors get it wrong far more often than they get it right.

The market and individual stocks react to events. Prices go up and down based on the news. The reason it's called "news" is because it hasn't happened yet. If you're trying to predict what a stock or the market will do tomorrow based on what it did yesterday, you're playing a fool's game. Remember the disclaimers you've read or heard about in ads touting investments? "Past performance is not an indicator of future returns" or some variation on that theme. Nothing and no one can predict the market, but that doesn't mean your retirement coach doesn't have some plays you can make in the market as part of your winning retirement game plan.

The Stock Market Goes Up over Time

The stock market may go up, but what goes up must come down from time to time.

Your coach has studied the tendencies of the market and knows that it's a great place for you to accumulate wealth that can, over time, form a large portion of your retirement nest egg. Your coach also knows that there will be major "corrections" in the market on occasion, and the very real potential exists for you to lose a significant portion of your market investment, all at once, during one of those events described earlier.

You can't keep the market from going up over the course of a decade, and you can't keep it from correcting from time to time. No one can. It's just a fact of life for stock market investors. When you might suffer a big loss is far more important than the loss itself.

If you're forty-five and you lose a significant chunk of your portfolio due to a stock market correction, that's a bad day. The happy fact is that you're likely to make up that loss (and then some) before you retire. You have time to recover (probably fifteen or twenty years) before you reach the point in your life when it's time to stop working so hard and earn new money.

If the correction happens when you're sixty-five, and if you have all or most of your portfolio in the market, there's a good chance you might not make up that loss. You just don't have the runway in terms of years to wait for your portfolio to recover.

The US stock market is the greatest wealth-creating engine ever known to man. I'm a big believer in it, and I think everyone should have money in the market throughout their lives. During the accumulation phase of your retirement game plan, the stock market might well be the star player on your bench. That said, when it's time to retire, it's best to keep a pretty low percentage of your nest egg in the active market. You're entering the distribution phase, during which you'll no longer be contributing new money to your portfolio. Your portfolio will be paying you on a regular basis and fueling your American Dream retirement.

Stocks are stars during your accumulation phase, but when the market corrects, it's almost like your star player suddenly switches sides and starts playing against you. You can beat them, though, if you anticipate this tendency and if your retirement coach has drawn up a smart game plan to begin stepping down your riskier investments as you get closer to retirement age.

Taxes and Prices Go Up over Time Too

Taxes and inflationary prices are two of the burliest defenders waiting to sack your retirement. Both are directly tied to actions taken by various parts of the government.

At the time of this writing, we have a federal government in the United States that is growing rapidly and expanding spending programs at an unprecedented rate. Reasonable people can disagree on whether these expansions are necessary, or even worthwhile, but the impact they have on retirees is clear and predictable.

Your retirement coach has studied the tendencies of these opponents too and knows that expansion of the government leads inexorably to higher taxes (to pay for those expanded programs) and higher rates of inflation (as businesses of all sizes raise prices to cover their new and rapidly growing costs due to higher taxes and expensive measures needed to comply with new regulations). Since the US government is designed in such a way that voters can theoretically change its direction every two to four years, these opponents can be stronger or weaker at different times during your retirement planning years. Spending and taxes can be cut, and monetary or economic policies can be changed to slow (or even stop) the growth of inflation. When an elected government takes full advantage of its power to rapidly expand, retirees can expect to pay more for everything from gasoline to eggs, and they can expect to have less money left after taxes to pay those higher prices.

By the way, all of these opponents are interrelated as members of the same team. News of changes in government policies can greatly affect the stock market too, driving down stock prices or keeping the market stagnant when it might otherwise be rocketing higher. Being aware of these opposing players and anticipating their tendencies is a crucial part of a winning retirement game plan. That's why having a coach who's studied these players and their tendencies is such a nice benefit to those playing (and planning to win) the retirement game.

Social Security

Your Social Security checks are likely to be major players on your bench. You might liken them, however, to players who are constantly griping to their agents about wanting to be traded or looking for a way to quit the game altogether.

The societal and governmental changes we discussed in the previous section have an impact on Social Security too. As described in chapter 3, unemployment and underemployment (represented by large numbers of people who have part-time jobs or low-income positions when they could be earning much more money) are big problems these days. The impact of these particular opponents is that fewer taxpayers are paying fewer tax dollars today to support the promise made to Social Security recipients who have been planning for years to rely on those checks.

Here's another fact of which many people are not aware: Social Security survivor benefits are not what you might think. Take the case of a retired couple composed of a husband who's worked a long professional career, and a wife who's raised the kids and kept the household, while occasionally holding down a job whenever her already-hectic schedule permitted. The husband is likely to have earned a higher monthly Social Security check than the wife did over the course of their careers. While they're both alive, the couple gets both checks. When one dies, the surviving spouse gets the larger of the two checks each month—but only that one check. I've worked with countless widows over the years who have been left with a real mess when their husbands die, and the couple had been relying heavily on their Social Security benefits in retirement.

Your coach has studied the tendencies and is eager to come up with the right game plan for you to endure whatever changes may be on the horizon with regard to Social Security. You don't have to pin your hopes of victory on these iffy players on your bench.

How's Your Health?

Eventually—hopefully many years from now—your own body will become an opponent in the retirement game. While your health and vitality might be good today, at some point your body's physical mechanisms will start acting like aggressive players on the other team. Recall Andy Rooney's quote from a previous chapter: "The idea of living a long life appeals to everyone, but the idea of getting old doesn't appeal to anyone." Ask any insurance salesman to check his mortality tables, and he'll have to report that, in the fullness of time, mortality is running a steady 100 percent.

We'll all be bound for our reward at some point, but for many of us, the end of the road will be marred by illness, disability, loss of vitality, and the eventual inability to take care of ourselves. People who study these things have identified a half dozen or so "activities of daily living" that we all do without thinking when we're young but which become difficult (maybe even impossible) as we age. These include things like being able to get in and out of a chair or the bed, toileting, taking care of personal hygiene, walking, climbing stairs, getting dressed, and feeding ourselves. Not to be a downer here, but at some point, there's a strong chance you'll lose the ability to do all or part of this list. When that happens, you need care, and that's why your retirement coach is likely to recommend the smart play of securing long-term care (LTC) insurance when you're still young enough to get good rates. Once you start losing those daily activities, you won't be able to get LTC insurance at any price. So it's smart to get it put in place as early as you can.

Occasionally, I run into folks who don't think LTC is important. "Won't Medicare or Medicaid take care of that when the time comes?" they ask. You don't want to rely on government programs for long-term care. In most cases those benefits don't kick in until you're well past the point of needing them—and they're temporary. The point of these programs is generally rehabilitation, with the expectation that you'll recover and get back to doing your daily activities of living. For many of us, though, that won't be the case, and our government benefits will expire before our health woes do.

Your retirement coach is likely to recommend some kind of LTC policy, to keep you from having to rely on the government, or, even worse, on your family members, who will often have to put their lives on hold to care for you. You might think you won't be any trouble, but trust me, caring for even the most patient and loving relative is a tough, often thankless, job.

Real Estate

In many cases, real estate is one of a retired couple's biggest financial assets. It's the three-hundred-pound star lineman on the bench. If owning that player truly makes you happy, then by all means hang on to the house—and your vacation property too. Again, every American Dream retirement is different, and I've had clients who didn't mind doing chores and repairs around the house; in fact, they found great satisfaction in doing them.

Still, when you retire, it's time to think about whether that's really you.

Real estate is both an asset and a liability. Take the case of a retired couple who had decided to keep their house but then a nefarious person sued them, claiming to have slipped on ice on their property, becoming disabled. Even if you find out the claim is a scam, and even if you discover that the perpetrator has done this sort of thing before, you still have to hire an attorney, go to court, and defend yourself. That's expensive and time-consuming, and not the kind of thing the overwhelming majority of my clients want to be busy with in retirement.

If you have a second home, it might be smart to pay someone to watch over it and even to act as the landlord or property manager if you rent it out during times you don't use it. Most of the time that kind of arrangement works just fine. I did come across a case during the recent pandemic in which a second-home tenant decided to stay well past the end of their rental ("I have nowhere else to go!") and, thanks to pandemic-related rules, got away without paying rent for months. Essentially, this guy had taken over rental property without paying a dime. Guess who still has to pay the property taxes, and guess who's still liable in case someone slips on ice there.

For these reasons, I'm not a fan of holding on to much real estate in retirement. In my experience, folks live a happier, more peaceful life in retirement when they don't have these real estate concerns to worry about. Your "forever home" and your vacation home can be nice players on your own bench, but when they start acting like opponents to your bliss, there's no shame in selling. Your retirement coach can make that part of your winning game plan.

* * *

One more cautionary tale, this one about a man who wanted to retire at seventy, and had every possibility of doing so, but had been playing as his own retirement opponent for a few years.

"Earl" had been helping his daughter by giving her money—and plenty of it—from his retirement nest egg. Maybe he thought this was necessary; it's certainly a kind-hearted thing to do. The daughter lived in a $650,000 house and could have earned more money on her own, which led me to believe that her dad was enabling her too much. He was taking money out of his own retirement fund, paying stiff taxes on that money, and giving it to her on a regular basis.

Earl came to me at age sixty-seven and stated his desire to retire at seventy. After running the numbers and putting together his best possible game plan, I had to tell him he would be retiring at age seventy-three instead. Maybe three more years on the job doesn't sound so bad when you're in your forties or fifties. But in your seventies, that can feel like a long sentence you've imposed on yourself, simply by enabling a family member.

Helping family members is one thing many retirees want to do, and I'm all for it if it will make my clients happier. Pay for weddings or college. Send grads on the trip of a lifetime before they start their careers. Help younger folks get out of a jam, especially if the jam seems temporary. When you're retiring, it's time to take a hard look at some of these difficult decisions and evaluate what help is worthwhile, and what really isn't.

Even if you're tempted to be your own opponent in retirement, like Earl, this is an opponent your retirement coach has studied. I understand and can anticipate this tendency on the part of some of my clients, and I can often help them game plan for retirement victory anyway.

My clients are dear to me, and the things they bring me aren't problems but puzzles that can be solved and planned for. That's my attitude—always has been, always will be. In the next chapter, we'll look at the difference this attitude can make.

5

ACHIEVING SUCCESS TOGETHER

In the movie *Moneyball,* Brad Pitt plays Billy Beane, a former baseball player who's now the general manager of a small-market major league team (the Oakland Athletics). The team enjoys strong talent and some recent success, including playoff appearances. They end up losing in the playoffs and not making it to the World Series. Beane realizes it's because he has a payroll budget less than a third of that of his chief rival, the New York Yankees. He just can't compete for the best high-dollar players. The Yankees lure away his star players with more money and end up gutting his team, and he's unsuccessful in attaining more funds from the club's owner. Beane knows he has to play the baseball management game in a very different way if he's to give his team a chance to be more successful.

Beane hires a math whiz, an economics grad from Yale (played by Jonah Hill), and uses statistics to identify a team of winning players he can afford—players other teams overlook because of traits the traditional, old-school coaches and scouts deem "defects." Eventually, Beane's team of misfits gets back to the playoffs after setting a record for the most consecutive wins in a season. At first, his own traditional, old-school coaches and scouts resist the change at every turn. Beane has to shake things up by trading players and firing some scouts. For the new game plan to work, Beane knows that he needs committed people who understand the plan, believe in it, and get that the club is now going to go about things in a revolutionary new way.

Different Coach, Different Approach

Billy Beane and his math-whiz assistant took an approach to baseball management that no one had tried before, and they changed not only baseball but all of professional sports in the process. Except they didn't do it by themselves. They needed that buy-in from everyone else in the organization—from the scouts to the game manager to the lowest-paid player.

In one key scene, an older star player tells Beane, "I've never seen a GM who talked to players like that." Beane replies, "You've never seen a GM who *was* a player."[1] Maybe that's why Beane eventually got that all-important buy-in at every level of the organization. He had been a player and a scout, so he could relate to his team members in ways other general managers would struggle to do.

---

1   Miller, Bennett. 2011. *Moneyball*. Columbia Pictures.

His approach was novel, but Beane's triumph depended on an age-old attitude that makes any approach perform at its best: achieving success together. At Tondryk Wealth Management, we're a little like the Billy Beane of financial advisors. We're like the GM who was a player and a scout. We take an approach that differs from what a lot of other fine, smart advisors take, and one of the central tenets of that approach is that we share life together with our clients.

We get to know our clients on a personal level, which is something many advisors from large firms don't have time to do. When someone in a client's family passes away, for instance, ours is often one of the first condolence calls that client will receive. We cheer for their kids' ball teams, we attend their family weddings, and we're delighted to hear about the arrival of new bundles of joy. From the cheers to the tears, we make it obvious that our clients aren't just portfolios or numbers to us.

We're a bit different from most other advisors in that we relate to our clients on a personal basis. We wouldn't have it any other way.

Focusing on "Transition Time"

We have great respect for other financial advisors, most of whom focus on their clients' portfolios during the accumulation phase of their lives. Those are the kind of advisors whose primary approach is to help their clients accumulate as much wealth as possible during their working years. Returning to our sports metaphor, they're kind of like the scouts on your retirement team, looking to help you assemble the best players you can with the money you have to save and invest before retirement.

At Tondryk Wealth Management, another way we're different is that our focus is on that crucial transition between the accumulation phase and the distribution phase of your retirement plan. That's the transition from the time when you're paying money into your retirement investments to the time when your investments pay you and fuel your American Dream retirement.

We love to meet new clients when they're a few years away from retirement, they've been saving what they could (and probably working with an accumulation advisor), and they've arrived at the point where it's time to put those players to work. Liquidity, safety, and income are all elements that need to be cohesive, balanced, and synchronized with a beautiful game plan. (We love all sports, including synchronized swimming, and are big fans of Esther Williams.)

Our clients learn that it isn't enough just to chase returns. A client's accumulation advisor (or scout) might have done a great job putting them into strong, growing investments (finding them good players), but when it's time to make the transition from accumulation to distribution, it's time to move to a coach who specializes in that area. That's our sweet spot, and that's where our clients find we can add tremendous value to their plans for their specific American Dream retirement.

Puzzles, Not Problems

Every retiree or retiring married couple is different, and that means every American Dream retirement should be unique and specifically personalized to the client. Our different approach also emphasizes starting where you are and tailoring a game plan that perfectly fits your assets, your priorities, and your needs. As we like to put it, we don't deal with our clients' problems, but rather we solve puzzles for them.

Remember what it's like to assemble a jigsaw puzzle? You dump the pieces out on the table, and where do you start? You turn all the pieces face up so you can start to see the picture as it emerges. That's exactly what we do, metaphorically speaking, when we ask a lot of questions of our new or prospective clients. We want to get as clear a picture as possible of their expenses and planned expenditures, as well as every kind of asset or liability they have, from real estate and stock accounts to health plans and insurance.

The next phase of your jigsaw puzzle solution will be to put together the edge pieces first, to get a clear outline of what the parameters and limits will be. Same with your retirement game plan. We want to know all we can about your American Dream retirement, and what your best retirement will look like within the parameters and limits of your specific priorities, needs, resources, and dreams.

When our clients bring us folders full of raw data on their expenses, bank accounts, insurance policies, investments, and so forth, it feels to us a lot like that exciting moment when you dump all the pieces of a jigsaw puzzle on the table and start looking for how those pieces will fit together. We love it. We're especially fond of the ability to take those often-complex pieces and put them together into a synchronized game plan some clients have likened to "a masterpiece."

Buy-In Is Critical in Sports—and in Retirement

Back to *Moneyball*. One of the biggest opponents of Billy Beane's new approach was the team's game manager who refused to play the team the way Beane had designed it to be played. For instance, he didn't play the first baseman Beane had acquired for his ability to frequently get on base, preferring instead to play a player whose hitting wasn't as strong but who had more experience fielding first base. Beane eventually traded away the experienced first baseman, specifically to force the game manager to play the guy he wanted played.

What does this have to do with your retirement game plan? Everything. One big difference in our approach here at Tondryk Wealth Management is that we take the time to thoroughly explain a client's specific, unique game plan so they can believe in the plan and buy-in in the ways Beane's game manager didn't. Because, as the old saying goes, the plan will work, but only if you work the plan.

Beane figured this out nearly too late in the movie. At one point, he did sit down with his game manager and apologize for not bringing him into the process sooner. The two hadn't really collaborated on this groundbreaking new approach Beane had decided to take, and it nearly wiped out the team's chances for success. We certainly get this. Experience has shown that when our clients collaborate with us on creating their retirement game plan, they understand it thoroughly and they buy in to how the plan will work for them.

I recently met with a prospective client who had heard my radio program and wanted more information. It soon became apparent that this gentleman, who had plenty of players (i.e., money) to play with, was determined to "do-it-himself" for the most part. He would let us create a game plan for him, but I didn't get the sense that he was going to play the game the way it would be designed to be played. That's okay. There's no harm in getting to know each other, but this fellow and I just weren't a good fit together.

By contrast, I had another extremely intelligent client not long ago who started out with the same basic skepticism about trusting his solid retirement game plan. He kept getting tempted to play things differently from the way they were set up. Eventually, we were able to achieve that all-important buy-in; we asked him what would happen to his wife if he passed away, given that she didn't have any experience working with the couple's finances. She would not be comfortable with a DIY approach. That was an eye-opener for him.

I'm happy to say he's working his plan quite nicely these days, and his plan is working quite nicely for him and his wife.

* * *

The transition from accumulation to distribution is an exciting time for any retiree or retiring couple, but it can also be extremely scary. We get it. When you have a coach with a lot of experience, tons of know-how, and a laser-like focus on helping you with exactly this phase of your retirement game plan, things get less scary in a hurry.

6

TERRIFYINGLY EXHILARATING

Imagine for a moment that you're a rookie running back in the National Football League. Let's say you had a decent college career—decent enough for a professional team to draft you—but you went later in the draft (Round Six). Now, all the summer practices and all your training in the weight room are about to be put to the test as you step on the field for the first time in the uniform of your new professional team.

In Tokyo.

Yes, your team is one of two selected to introduce NFL football to Japan, so you and your teammates flew eighteen hours to get there, you did a couple of light practices under the influence of jet lag (a phenomenon with which you're not familiar), and now you're about to play the game "for real." Even though it's only a preseason game, everything counts. Especially for you, as a rookie, who has virtually no shot at being the team's starting back and may not even make the team at all. Your future depends on what you show your coaches during this one game.

Screw up during this game, and there may not be another. Every Monday, the team has to cut some guys from the roster, and every rookie knows well that they might be next on the chopping block. You don't get to play your customary running back position during this game. You're just in there on "special teams," trying to cover punts and kickoffs, running full bore down the field to try to tackle the other poor rookie who just caught the kickoff and is also worried about making his team's roster.

The kick is in the air, and you start running.

Imagine how you would feel at that moment. You've been playing the game your whole life, since you were a kid, and though you're still "on the bubble" to make the team, you've earned the right to be on that bubble. Hundreds of other guys would love to be in your position. You know this—it makes sense intellectually—but how do you *feel*, now that everything counts?

Exhilarated, probably. But also, certainly *terrified*.

There's nothing for it now but to remember your technique, trust your game plan, and focus on your objective.

That feeling of "terrified exhilaration" is very familiar to us here at Tondryk Wealth Management. That's because a large percentage of our clients have told us they feel the same way as they approach their retirement date. They knew having the opportunity to retire would be exciting. It's something they've worked hard to have the right to do (not unlike our young running back). It's also scary.

After all, no matter when or how we finally retire from our working careers, we're all rookies stepping out onto the field of retirement for the first time. That's why the folks who retire best are the ones who have a good coach and a solid game plan. They're ready to tackle retirement head-on, so to speak. Intellectually, they know their plan is going to work, and they're going to be okay (or far better than okay).

It's still terrifyingly exhilarating. Everyone gets to this terrifyingly exhilarating moment, when it's time to kick off their retirement and all the game planning and preparation are about to be put to the test "for real." It's an emotional time for everyone.

That's why we keep a box of tissues in our office.

The Power of the Plan

Many decisions a person makes purely on emotion tend to work out differently from the way the person intended. Don't get me wrong; some decisions should include a healthy dose of emotion, such as the decision to marry (and whom to marry) or to have children. Some decisions require faith, and faith isn't exactly logical. According to the wise philosopher Voltaire, "Faith consists in believing when it is beyond the power of reason to believe." So since we know things like faith and emotion are involved with most big life decisions—including when and how to retire—we keep the tissues handy.

Just as the rookie football player has endured hundreds of grueling practices and watched hours and hours of film to prepare for the big game, your retirement coach has done the work to prepare you for this moment. You have a game plan. A winning game plan. We worked together, you and I, to solve the puzzle of how your American Dream retirement was going to work. We know the plan will work, if you work the plan.

That's the beauty of the retirement game plan. It's quantitative, well-thought-out, and based on detailed conversations during which you and I worked together to create it. It makes sense and anticipates every next move the market, or the government, might make. That gives you the confidence to make solid decisions, even when things get emotional.

One of the big worries that characterizes the emotional impact of retiring is the concern over running out of money. Our clients know that, with their retirement game plan to guide their decisions through this exciting and scary time, we won't let that happen to them.

* * *

"Lou" came to see us when his time to retire was drawing near. He had worked for years starting and building a successful business, and now the plan called for the sale of that business to provide a big part of the financial fuel for his and his wife's American Dream retirement.

Intellectually, Lou knew this was his next move. Emotionally, it wasn't easy for him. After all, a great deal of Lou's self-perception, and especially his sense of self-worth, was tied up in that business. In retirement, Lou would have the chance to spend his hours and days doing the things he loved: golfing, traveling, working around the house, and playing with his grandkids. Lou was likely to struggle a bit, especially at first, to "find himself" in those activities. For years, Lou has been a businessman. That's how he identifies himself. It's how he knows who he is. He's not a golfer, a traveler, a handyman, or a babysitter. Lou is a businessman. Once he sells the company, Lou is doing nothing less than letting go of a substantial piece of his self-identification.

These days, retirees of both genders are dealing with the emotions associated with leaving behind careers they worked hard to build. For several generations, this was especially tough for men. Fifty years ago, if a man found himself socializing at, say, a cocktail party, the first question he would ask, and answer, when meeting a man for the first time would be, "So what do you do?" And his wife, upon meeting another wife for the first time, would certainly hear, "So what does your husband do?"

I'm sure some of these questions would have felt like interrogations, but most of the time the question was just an icebreaker: What do you "do" to earn the money to support your family and your lifestyle? Tell me about yours, and I'll tell you about mine. We identify ourselves by the work we do. It's emotional. That's what makes the transition into retirement so difficult for many people, and Lou was no different. But he had a game plan for this transition, and it was a good one. So when the time came, Lou could rely on his game plan to give him the confidence and courage to make the right decisions around selling his company and moving into the next phase of his long and happy life.

Exciting, yes. For many like Lou, also very scary. Terrifyingly exhilarating!

* * *

"Donna" had a similar level of emotion when she came to see us near retirement time, though her circumstances were quite different. She had worked for many years for a large corporation, and she had always known there would come a day when she could close the book on that brilliant career and begin living her American Dream retirement. No less than Lou, Donna associated herself and her sense of who she was with her work. Letting go of her career would have to be something done just right, at just the right time, and with just the right game plan for retirement.

She had been collaborating with us on solving her particular retirement puzzle for a few years, but as we met to catch up and make any necessary adjustments to her plan, well, she needed the tissue.

As described in the previous chapter, we share life with our clients. Donna was a client but also something of a friend. It was quite natural for her to talk with us not just about the numbers and the timelines but about the emotions that drove her motivations. It turns out "Corporate" had given Donna a new boss not long ago, and this boss's idea of leadership was to berate and yell at longtime trusted managers like Donna.

"I've loved my job for many years, and I've grown in it. I'm a respected manager and a strong leader," Donna told us. "Now I'm really starting to hate even going there."

But retire? Was she really ready to make that big leap of faith? It was all quite terrifyingly exhilarating for Donna too.

You can probably guess what happened next. We took another detailed look at Donna's retirement game plan, ran the numbers, and found we were able to tell her she didn't have to keep working at a job she had come to hate. She put in her retirement notice the next day. Now, when Donna bumps into a new acquaintance at a cocktail party, if they ask her what she does, she can say she plays bridge, she sings in the church choir, and she's slowly seeing the entire world, one trip at a time.

Oh, and if she feels like it, she can throw "I'm a retired manager" in there too.

* * *

The discussion about when and how to "pull the trigger" on retirement can be emotional and terrifyingly exhilarating for couples too. "Mike" and "Cathy" are one such couple we know.

Cathy retired a few years ago from a long and successful career as a government attorney, and now she pulls in a nice pension check (remember those?), along with her Social Security payments. Her law license is still active, so Cathy also takes on the occasional case for a small government client who just can't seem to let her go. In the course of her career, she made some good investments and also inherited a bit of money from her parents.

Halfway through that career, she met and married Mike, for whom it was a second marriage. Mike's career ("I'm not sure you could call it a *career*," he says) was completely different. He had supported his first wife and four kids as a stage actor and singer, and also by working as a writer, editor, and ad guy for various newspapers between theater productions. His kids are all grown now, but Mike is still working—and working hard—running a copywriting business.

Cathy always had a retirement plan, based on what she knew she could expect from her government pension. So far that plan is working out fine for her, financially speaking. Mike's retirement plan had always been to work until he died, unless one of his novels made the best seller list. Not really a plan at all. The emotion around the couple's retirement situation is strong. Like Lou, Mike's not sure he's ready to let go of his work and the feeling of self-worth he's derived from finally building a successful business and not having to rely on the next audition for a paycheck. But Cathy, having made different choices early in her career, is already retired and, as she puts it, doesn't "have anyone to play with."

Again, you can probably guess the happy outcome. The puzzle Cathy and Mike need to solve in order to have their American Dream retirement together is nothing that a solid retirement game plan can't solve. Once the plan is in place and the numbers are understood, the couple can move past the terrifyingly exhilarating questions about retirement with the confidence that their plan will work.

* * *

I don't know for sure how our rookie running back felt at that key moment in his first preseason game, many years ago, in Tokyo. I can only guess that he was terrifyingly exhilarated. I do know that he had a great coach who provided him and the rest of his team with a solid game plan. Not only did the team win that preseason game, but they went on to play in the NFL playoffs several years in a row, and that run included two Super Bowl championships.

I also know that our rookie player, armed perhaps with the confidence that only comes from solid preparation and good planning, ran down the field and made an impressive tackle on that first kickoff play. It was the kind of tackle that got him noticed in an exceedingly positive way. One veteran teammate later said, "Wow, look at the rookie! That's when we knew he was really a football player."

He sure was!

I also know, as do many NFL fans, what happened to our rookie during his career. He made the team during his rookie season, and he climbed the depth chart to become the starting running back on a team whose offense depended on a solid running game. He went to the playoffs with his team—some say he carried the team into and through the playoffs—and by the time he retired from playing football, he had amassed many honors. He was one of only a handful of backs who had rushed for two thousand yards in a single season, and he was named MVP of both the Super Bowl and the NFL as a whole.

That's the football story of Terrell Davis, who wore number 30 for the Denver Broncos in the late 1990s. From that terrifyingly exhilarating first preseason kickoff, all the way through his chance to hoist the Super Bowl trophy, Davis showed what hard work, ingenuity, courage, and a little luck can accomplish on the gridiron. Davis has said many times that he had a wonderful career he could have only dreamed of.

Your retirement story can be similar. Get a great coach and a solid game plan, and you'll have the confidence to achieve your own American Dream retirement.

If you're reading this, the ball is likely in the air, and it's time to start running toward that dream.

7
THREE "INVESTMENT WORLDS"

We've all seen the shows and movies that depict the tough-but-brilliant coach standing at a chalkboard, drawing up plays, his players watching in eager anticipation. John Wooden used to do this. So did Vince Lombardi, Knute Rockne, and just about every successful sports coach you can think of.

These days the ol' chalkboard has gone out of style, but the historic principle is still the same: A great coach will use whatever means he or she can to teach players exactly how they can win whatever game they're playing and beat whatever opponent they're up against. Once players understand how their game plan can work, they're easier to motivate. They can more readily be inspired to go, fight, and win!

Your retirement coach (that's me) takes a similar approach with clients and prospective clients (that might be you). No, I don't drag out an old-school chalkboard, but I do use the modern-day equivalent of the whiteboard to illustrate for my players exactly how their retirement game plan is going to work for them. It's true—I'll draw up the plays for you, right before your very eyes.

What my clients learn during these meetings (really, coaching sessions) often surprises them. Many people come to retirement age believing they only have two basic plays they can run with their investments: They can go for broke (in some cases, literally) and invest in high-risk, high-growth instruments, or they can play it safe (literally playing not to lose) and keep their nest egg in products that offer low (or no) risk or growth. Having some money in each of these categories is what many people consider "investment diversity," or having a diversified portfolio.

My idea of a diversified portfolio is quite different.

It's true that most financial advisors will lead you to believe that there are really two phases of your investment life. There's the accumulation phase, during which the high-growth products make more sense because you need to accumulate a nest egg. You're younger and have time to recover the inevitable losses. Then there's the distribution phase, where you essentially stop growing your retirement fund and it starts to pay you.

Knute Rockne might have said you can either "run it left or run it right," but in the retirement investment game, there's a third play you can make. It helps our clients win their American Dream retirements—and win big-time.

The Three "Worlds" of Investing

Imagine you're sitting in my office, ready to see what plays I can draw up specifically for you. First, I'll ask you what would make this a great meeting for you, and then I'll use a tried-and-true questionnaire to guide me in asking you a bunch of questions. I want to know everything about your situation, financially speaking—akin to a sports coach finding out what her players are capable of doing on the field or on the court.

Once I have a clear picture of your situation and what victory would look like for you, it's time to draw up the game plan. I spring to the whiteboard and draw three columns representing the three investment worlds in which you can play the retirement game.

First, we discuss the left-hand column, which I label "Safe Money." This is the play-not-to-lose investment world, where you would have your money in certificates of deposit (CDs), money market funds, treasuries, fixed annuities, your checking and savings accounts, and other such low- or no-risk (and low- or no-growth) financial instruments.

Next, we jump over to the right-hand column, which I label "At Risk." This is the "throw-the-ball-deep" investment world, where you would invest in things like stocks, exchange-traded funds (ETFs), some types of bonds and mutual funds, and variable annuities. Here we would talk about the high-growth and high-risk products many new clients have used in the past to accumulate their nest egg. At this point, I must go for absolute clarity on one key point. At the bottom of this right-hand, at-risk column, I write and underline, "Your principal is not protected."

I'll then return to the safe-money left-hand column and make a note that your money in this investment world is protected. Most of these investments are "liquid," which means you can get at it when you need it. (Fixed annuities may have a surrender charge before their maturity date.) I like to advise folks to keep about six months of expenses in this investment world because, in life, stuff happens. You might need to buy or repair a car or make repairs or improvements to your home. It's important to have some cash on hand when you need new tires or a new roof, and it's also important to replenish your safe-money accounts once you've tapped them for these necessary expenditures.

Your money is protected in that left-hand column, but it's no longer growing.

Many advisors will insist you keep money in both the left- and right-hand columns. I think clients should always have money in both columns. They should run their game plan as though they're happy to run the ball conservatively, so to speak, but they also have that "deep threat" available to them.

That said, when it's time to transition from accumulation to distribution—our specialty here at Tondryk Wealth Management—it's time to move a substantial part of your retirement fund into the center of our whiteboard. After all, suppose you have the lion's share of your money in the go-for-broke investment world of high growth and high risk, meaning most of your money is invested in the Wall Street casino. The market grows over time, of course, but it also corrects at times. So what will happen to your nest egg when the market experiences a 30 percent correction (which at some point it will)? If you're forty, you can recover that loss. If you're sixty, your chances are much slimmer. If you're eighty, you aren't going to make that money back.

The "Magical" Middle World

What if you could have the best of both worlds: protection and growth? Investors and retirees—as well as their advisors and coaches—have been asking that question for years. And today, there's a great answer: Pretty much, you can have it both ways.

I label the middle column on our whiteboard "Linked Accounts." These are instruments similar to products in both of the other investment worlds, but they form a bridge that connects protection with modest growth. Linked accounts are products such as linked CDs, linked treasuries, and perhaps the crown jewel, linked or "fixed index" annuities. We call them "linked" because that's exactly what they are—they're linked to the equity market in such a way that they can take advantage of growth when the market is up, but they don't depreciate when the market goes down. A fixed index annuity works similarly to the way a pension plan works in that you're creating a lifelong income stream for you and your spouse. At the bottom of the linked accounts column, I write and underline "Your principal is protected."

It's important to note that your money in this investment world is not going to realize huge gains or grow at a rapid rate. It's going to give you modest growth. At this key transition phase, that's all you need. The risk you leave behind while still capturing that modest growth makes the linked accounts investment world almost magical for folks seeking their American Dream retirement.

When you're still younger and in your working years, you want to have six months' worth of expenses in the safe-money world and the bulk of your investments in the go-for-broke (high-growth and high-risk) world. You're in the accumulation phase of your retirement investment. Once you transition to the distribution phase, you want to keep some money in that high-growth column but move much of it from that column into the "magic" middle column to take advantage of the protected growth that linked accounts offer.

Planning for Five Games

Another truth that often surprises clients who are just starting to investigate their retirement possibilities is that, really, you need not just one solid game plan, but five. The first is income planning. Most people understand that all-important safe-money investment world, and they know that they're going to have to have income during retirement. They'll no longer be receiving paychecks but will need "playchecks" in order to live the American Dream retirement they've worked so hard to earn.

The second is investment planning. Most clients are also comfortable with that go-for-broke, high-growth, high-risk investment world. After all, that's where they've been playing throughout their careers. They may not know how to play well in that right-hand column once they are no longer earning new money, but most have a sense that they should not stop investing and trying to grow their wealth.

Third is tax planning. This one is often overlooked. There are many things your retirement coach can suggest that will help reduce your tax burden. Remember, Uncle Sam is your partner in retirement and has to be paid. He's also one of your most formidable opponents in the retirement game. A good retirement game plan will not only provide for income and investment but for minimizing (legally) your tax liability.

Fourth is health care planning. Many people enter retirement feeling healthy and robust. For that reason, you can easily overlook the notion that you won't always feel that way. As we discussed in earlier chapters, it's a sad fact that we start to lose vitality as we age. A good retirement plan takes this into account and provides plays you can make to provide for your health care in your golden years. An LTC insurance program is a wise choice for most retirees and essential for many.

Fifth and final is legacy planning. It's another sad fact that, in the fullness of time, mortality is running at 100 percent. A great retirement plan also makes provisions for what will happen to your money after you leave all three investment worlds, so to speak.

Given the need to plan for all five of these retirement game plans, it's crucially important to have a coach who can tailor your American Dream retirement, draw on the player strengths you bring, and help you take advantage of all three investment worlds.

* * *

Because it's so essential to a successful transition from accumulation to distribution, let's next spend a little more time on that magical middle column, the linked accounts investment world. We want to develop a more thorough understanding of the annuity products that make this investment world so powerful for folks who want an American Dream retirement.

8

SECURING AN INCOME

Hoosiers is a great movie about overcoming adversity, intimidation, and fear. If you're a basketball fan, you probably already know this. In the film, Gene Hackman plays a high school basketball coach who takes his small-town Indiana team to the state championship. He knows the big-city venue will intimidate the boys, and so will the crowd that will be many times bigger than any they had ever seen before.

Talk about terrifyingly exhilarated.

So before they board the bus for the city, the coach takes the boys into their home gymnasium and has them measure the court: how far it is from the free-throw line to the goal, how wide and high the basket is, how wide and long the court is, everything. Then, when they arrive in Indianapolis for the big tournament, he has them perform the same measurements on the court on which they'll play the championship game, and they find that the measurements are exactly the same as those they recorded on their home court.

The coach doesn't have to say a word, but he can see that the implication of this exercise is dawning on his players and that their fear is melting away. "There's no reason you can't do here exactly what you did at home: Win."[2]

As a retirement coach, I love seeing the fear melt away from my clients when I take them through the "width and breadth" of what they can accomplish within that magical middle column described in the previous chapter.

The type of linked account known as a "fixed index annuity" is almost magical in its power to melt the fear away from my clients who have heard too much about annuities to approach the topic with an open mind. Folks aren't wrong when they say they've heard bad things about annuities. As we'll demonstrate, not all annuities are alike, and some just aren't a good idea for most people entering retirement. Many people don't know what kind of annuities exist in that middle world we've described, and when they learn about them, you can almost see their fear evaporate.

"Mary" was one such client. She had had a good career and accumulated a nice nest egg. She came to see me after hearing my radio program. I wasn't long into my coaching session when Mary folded her arms and sat back. "If this is about annuities, I'm just not

---

[2] Anspaugh, David. 1986. *Hoosiers*. Hemdale Film Corporation.

interested," she said. Of course, my policy is always to hear a client out and to make sure I understand the terrifyingly exhilarated emotions they're dealing with. As I listened to Mary, it was obvious she had been visualizing a difficult and scary retirement, as we described in chapter 1. In Mary's mind, retirement was likely to be more about babysitting than traveling, more about leftovers than country-club cuisine. She knew a lot about annuities—as they existed several years ago, when variable annuities were a hot commodity and many people lost a lot of money because they trusted salespeople who offered such products.

As I explained the sort of annuities I advocate (the kind that can create a solid income stream in retirement without the risk of losing your principal), I saw the same thing in Mary that I had seen in countless clients over the years.

Her fear just melted away.

It turns out that the "hoop" representing a retirement income she could count on wasn't as high or as small or as far away as she had been led to believe. I'm pleased to say Mary is now enjoying her American Dream retirement, fueled in no small part by the kind of annuity she had no idea was available to her today. She spends time with her grandkids, to be sure, but she also spends a lot of happy time on cruise ships.

Not All Annuities Are the Same

The overwhelming majority of folks who come into my office for help with their retirement planning are relieved when they see what they could accomplish with a solid retirement plan. Almost all are happy to run the plays I draw up, once they've had a chance to understand the realities of the powerful tools available to them today.

"Annuities" is a term that has received a bad rap in recent years. There are at least four broad categories of annuities, and while some types of annuity are fully deserving of the bad reputation some people hold in their minds, others are not at all like the annuities they've heard about. Basically, an annuity is a contract between an individual and an insurance company that can offer income, potential growth, or both.

The four types of annuity are immediate, fixed, variable, and fixed index. The immediate annuity will pay you an ongoing income stream for a specific period of time, such as ten years or for a lifetime. The fixed annuity can be thought of as the "plain vanilla" type of annuity, where the insurance provider guarantees a certain rate of return (say, 3 percent) over a certain period of time (typically three to five years). In this example, if you take out a $100,000 fixed annuity paying 3 percent over three years, you'll have roughly $109,000 (plus compounding) after three years, at which time you can withdraw your money or renew the annuity at whatever interest rate the insurer is guaranteeing at that time. Interest rates can be very low with basic fixed annuities in today's low-interest environment, and you do have to make choices after each annuity period as to whether or not to renew. The fixed annuity can be a good investment vehicle, but it's in that left-hand column (the safe-money investment world) described in the previous chapter.

The variable annuity was extremely popular a few decades ago, particularly because salespeople could show phenomenal growth rates from the previous year and create the assumption that the fund would continue to grow at that sort of high rate indefinitely. Variable annuities are tied to the stock market (they're in that right-hand column, the "go-for-broke" investment world), and since the market does inevitably suffer corrections, those annuities can be vulnerable to significant losses. They're relatively risky. A variable annuity is basically a mutual fund in an annuity wrapper, and considering the fees that often accompany these instruments, variable annuities are generally quite expensive when compared with other options. I don't recommend them for my clients. It's the variable annuity that, more than the other types, has given annuities a poor, and mostly undeserved, reputation.

The fixed index annuity is our star player in the income game. A fixed index annuity is a sort of hybrid between a fixed annuity and a variable annuity. It's different from a fixed annuity in that a fixed index annuity has the potential for a higher rate of return. Meanwhile, the difference between a fixed index annuity and a variable annuity is that the principal and interest are protected from loss—the money is not in the stock market but linked to an index, such as the Standard & Poor's 500 (commonly known as the S&P 500). If the index goes up in a given year, depending on how your fixed index annuity is structured, your fund shares in that growth. If, on the other hand, the index is flat or even loses ground during the year, you don't suffer a loss—you just get a zero rate of return. The fixed index annuity is one of the big stars in that magical middle world of linked accounts described in chapter 7. Principal protected from loss, combined with a modest growth rate, give the fixed index annuity the ability to provide something like the best of both worlds when it comes to annuities.

As you can tell, these new fixed index annuities are different from annuities of the past, in some vitally important ways.

Not Your Grandfather's Annuity

What were your biggest fears when you visualized your retirement (as described in chapter 1)? Were you, like Mary, anxious about having enough money to live your American Dream retirement? Were you worried that old-school annuities might be your only option, despite the many horror stories you had heard about them? On the other hand, if you've been a conscientious saver throughout your career, did you have high hopes for the kind of retirement that would let you spend more time on cruise ships than on grandchildren-babysitting assignments?

That's what I love about fixed index annuities. They offer good growth potential and complete protection of your principal. In short, they're an excellent tool for creating income streams to fuel your American Dream retirement.

These are not your grandfather's annuities.

One couple who recently decided to work with my firm had done a good job saving throughout their working years, and they wanted to be able to have about $7,000 per month of income during their golden years. That's the income figure that would give them their true American Dream retirement. The couple's two Social Security checks combined would provide about half of that $7,000 figure, so they needed a game plan that would bring in the rest. The income stream we created with a fixed index annuity became the star player that filled the gap for them.

Whether it's $7,000 per month or some other figure, if you want to have a successful American Dream retirement, you have to make some provision for income.

Another couple came to me with a million dollars they had worked their whole lives to save. "This is it," they told me. "This is all we have, and it has to last us the rest of our lives. We absolutely can't lose it." They were extremely nervous—almost fearful—about the possibility of having their money invested in the Wall Street casino. They were quite relieved when I showed them a game plan that didn't require a big investment in the stock market at all. I established a fixed index annuity income stream for them, and they stand to get fairly decent growth in a good year. In a bad year, they won't lose a penny of their principal nor any of the interest they earned previously. They may not make a gain during that bad year, but over the course of their retirement, their growth will likely average a decent, modest return.

Not bad for a thoroughly protected income stream. These are just a couple of examples of scenarios we see all the time.

* * *

We all love market volatility when the market's shooting higher, but we can find ourselves crying in our milk when the inevitable corrections come. Gambling with a person's or couple's retirement nest egg is never a good strategy. Too much anxiety, too much out-and-out fear, and not enough optimism to "fuel the dream." Linked accounts, such as fixed index annuities, eliminate that fear because they keep things moving in a positive direction. All growth is good growth, even if it's modest growth over time—and no loss.

If you haven't seen *Hoosiers,* you'll be happy to learn that Gene Hackman's young dreamers did, in fact, become champions. Under his coaching, they were able to visualize victory. When things grew dimmer and fear began to rear its ugly head, he was able to help them overcome their terrified exhilaration and play well enough to hoist the state championship trophy.

Next, let's take a look at your game plan for making your exit from the workaday world and making a grand entrance into your American Dream retirement.

9
EXIT CARDS

Sports metaphors abound for this wonderful moment in your life—the moment when you get to finally retire from the tyranny of the Monday-morning alarm clock and the stress of working as hard as you always have. We've all seen the tearful goodbyes of major sports stars who have decided to hang up their cleats (or spikes, skates, or whatever footwear they've used throughout their pro career).

There are also examples of how good professional teams can close out their opponents and exit a game with a victory. The football team that has a good four-minute offense that can hold the ball (and the lead) to run out the clock on the other team. The baseball club that has a strong-pitching closer who can keep opponents from scoring runs in the ninth inning (or a cleanup hitter they can send to the plate when they're behind in the bottom of the ninth, hoping to smash a walk-off homer). The hockey team that's good at scoring an empty-net goal late in the third period to make sure their opponents can't skate off the ice with a comeback tie or win.

Another game that we now see on sports networks is competitive poker. I'm not sure there's a universal consensus on poker being a sport, per se, but it is a competition, and evidently enough people will stay up late at night to watch it on television to make it a viable programming choice for the sports networks. Maybe that's what "Jake," one of our favorite clients, was thinking about when he coined the term "exit cards" to describe the plans he had put in place to ensure he could retire from his working career on his own terms, no matter how the decision to retire were to come about.

I'm no gambler, so I'm not sure if there's a game plan for poker or a strategy for exiting the game. Jake's description of his exit cards was certainly something any retirement advisor would understand and appreciate. Jake had his eye on retirement throughout his working life, and he made choices earlier in his professional career that would cover all of what he called the "what-ifs": "What if I lose my job?" "What if I get sick or disabled?" "What if I get fed up and really want to quit?" No matter what came up, he wanted to be able to cash in his chips on his terms.

Jake had built up quite a jackpot by the time he was ready to play his exit cards. "When other people my age were paying for the latest phone or for cable TV, I was saving up for another exit card. I never had cable TV," Jake said.

Not everyone would want to live without things like cable television. I mean, how could they keep up with the latest poker tournament results if they didn't have the sports channels? Luckily, most people can build some nice "cards" they can play when they exit their working life and enter their American Dream retirement—even if they've paid for cable. One key to Jake's successful exit was that he had been able to identify things he didn't really need (like cable television) and save or invest the money he otherwise would have spent on those things. Jake was able to retire at fifty-eight with a wonderful nest egg to fuel his American Dream in his golden years.

When we help clients develop a solid retirement game plan that properly balances their portfolio with the right mix of the three investment worlds, they know they can lay down a winning hand when the time is right to cash in.

Debt as Wild Card

You might have a pretty strong hand at the poker table, but if your opponent ends up with a wild card they can use against you, it's much harder to scoop up the pot. Debt is one such wild card that a smart retiree will be well-advised to plan for.

I met "Gary" and "Tammy" some time ago, and I'll never forget Gary's despair as he began to talk about his situation and "lay his cards on the table." The couple were nearing retirement age, but they had three children either in college or ready to enter college, and a mountain of debt Gary was considering hiring a service to help him pay off.

The man sat in my office with his head in his hands. He and Tammy had no hand to play and no exit cards they could use to retire, until they faced the reality that they would have to pay off their debt. They weren't able to retire when they had wanted to, but as we worked together on a plan to gain and keep momentum in paying off their debt, the dark cloud that had been hanging over their heads began to clear. Gary and Tammy met with the Tondryk Wealth Management team on a regular schedule to make sure they were staying on track with their game plan and working their way out of debt.

Now, a few years later, I'm happy to say Gary doesn't have any reason to hang his head. The couple is in great financial shape; they're seeing a light at the end of the tunnel and a real chance at a great American Dream retirement.

Gary and Tammy offer just one example of the staunch opponent debt can represent to a retiring person or couple. When you're nearing retirement age, it's important to start creating a solid game plan for getting that wild card off the table. It starts by establishing a point beyond which you will stop (or significantly slow) your accumulation of new debt.

When a person or couple comes to me in their late fifties or early sixties, one question that almost always comes up is when and whether they should pay off their home mortgage. Some clients are curious about ads they've seen or heard regarding refinancing the home to get a lower interest rate. For some folks it makes sense to do this, but for many, refinancing at retirement age means you'll likely have a house payment for the rest of your life. Our main goal at this point in our clients' lives is to make sure they have a game plan that will guarantee them sufficient income for their American Dream retirement. When they're able to get rid of their house payment, that goal becomes much more attainable.

I do have clients who are continuing to make house payments during retirement, but I try to find ways to help them get their mortgages paid off earlier. One couple who married later in life immediately bought a house together, and while they're retired, they each make payments on the mortgage and that's just part of what they want to do together. Again, every American Dream retirement is different. For most clients, I try to help them make a game plan to pay off their house by the time they're around age sixty. If we can't do that, I at least want to see the mortgage wild card swept off the table by the time they're sixty-five.

It's a math puzzle. I try to help clients solve the equation of how much extra they should try to pay on their mortgage each month, especially while they're still working, to get their house paid off on the schedule that will allow them to retire when and how they really want to. A solid game plan guarantees their income and ensures they won't run out of money down the road.

Today's Wild Cards

The coronavirus pandemic of the last couple of years has certainly shaken things up for folks who are at or near retirement these days. Talk about a wild card! When large portions of the economy were shut down, work and careers changed for just about everybody (not just retirees). Many people lost jobs or businesses, and the relief programs that were offered weren't enough to save everyone's work or career.

The pandemic didn't help the overall personal debt situation in the United States either. In a sense, the pandemic's wild card added or exacerbated the debt wild card for far too many people. As things began to open back up, the pandemic threw another wild card on the table: vaccine mandates, issued by the government or by the companies for which many retirement-aged folks were still working.

"Randy" was a client of ours who had to deal with these wild cards as he was nearing his retirement. A brilliant engineer, Randy worked for a firm that issued a vaccine mandate to all its employees, and Randy couldn't comply. He had received a certain preventive medical treatment and couldn't receive the vaccine for ninety days thereafter, which would push him past the company's deadline for receiving either a vaccine or a pink slip.

A coworker met with Randy to confirm delivery of some material for a major project for which Randy was a key contributor. "Don't order this stuff," Randy told him. "I may not be here by the time it arrives." He explained his dilemma to his coworker, and it was a shock. "You have to be here!" was the reply. "We need you here for this project."

To make a long story short, when a cry went up from Randy's team about the possibility of losing him from the project, the firm found a way to grant their brilliant engineer an exemption, whether on religious grounds or for some other reason. Randy ended up with an acceptable outcome following this wild card, but many people didn't. Too many people had to accept a new reality that meant they either couldn't retire on their hoped-for schedule or couldn't see a time when they could retire at all.

There's always hope. Even if your opponents in the retirement game throw every wild card at you they can, you can likely still create some exit cards and a solid game plan for winning your American Dream retirement—even if it's not quite on the schedule you might have had before. You just need a good coach who can help you solve the puzzle as it exists today, in the aftermath of these new challenges.

One happy truth these wild cards haven't changed is this: Many people can still retire earlier and better than they imagined—once they have a strong game plan in place.

* * *

Whether you face new challenges brought on by the pandemic or you find yourself in debt over your head, these wild cards emphasize the most important lesson to people approaching their American Dream retirement: You must get your exit cards in place. The sooner, the better.

As we've discussed throughout the book, you have opponents in the retirement game, and they're going to get in the way of your American Dream retirement. They'll throw every wild card at you they can, in what often seems like a concerted effort to shake you up as you approach your sunset years. Yet, with a great game plan, you can be unbeatable. With a full hand of exit cards, your retirement can be unshakeable. Creating that unshakeable American Dream retirement game plan is what we're all about at Tondryk Wealth Management.

10
UNSHAKEABLE RETIREMENT

A team that has a superior collection of talented players and a solid game plan is hard to beat. If these elements are in place, as long as the team sticks to the game plan, they're practically unbeatable. Their opponents will have plans and designs of their own, of course. One of the big aims of your opponent in any game, including the retirement game, is to try to shake you out of your game plan. A train that stays on its tracks is virtually certain of reaching its destination. It's when the train gets off track that disaster can ensue (trains off their tracks almost always constitute disasters).

Another way to think of opponents is to imagine driving across a massive suspension bridge, like those you find in the New York or San Francisco areas. You would probably drive across to the other side without a care in the world, but imagine that same bridge without guardrails. Nothing between your vehicle and the deep blue ocean except your ability to stay in your lane. That would be a bit more exciting, wouldn't it? The last thing you would want as you drive across a suspension bridge is excitement. Certainty and assurance would be more preferred terms for what you want on that bridge.

In the movie *A League of Their Own,* Tom Hanks plays the role of a manager of a professional women's baseball team in the 1940s, when major league baseball was suspended due to the number of ball players who had to be overseas serving in the military. In one scene, Hanks's character visits the pitcher's mound and says, "The game's gettin' kinda exciting, isn't it?"[3]

He wasn't suggesting the excitement was a good thing. His team had the lead, and all he needed his pitcher to do was to throw strikes and get three batters out before the opponents could score runs and catch up. The pitcher was tired, and opposing batters were starting to get hits and threaten to score. What the manager wanted was some assurance, some certainty, that the game wouldn't get out of hand. What he was seeing, though, was excitement of the kind no baseball manager or sports coach wants to see.

As retirement coach for many cherished clients, I share Hanks's character's apprehension about this type of excitement. Once we've established a winning game plan for a client—a plan that gives certainty

---

[3] Marshall, Penny. 1992. *A League of Their Own.* Parkway Productions.

and assurance that the client will be able to win their particular American Dream retirement—we hope the client will stick to the plan. There are guardrails. There's a track. The last thing I want to see, metaphorically speaking, is a client getting derailed from their American Dream retirement or driving off the side of the bridge.

While the plan will certainly work, it only works if you stick to it. You can't let anything shake you loose from your plan. That's why we encourage clients to establish certain guardrails of their own and keep their retirement "unshakeable."

Balance Your Needs

As mentioned earlier, one of the things people look forward to when they close their eyes and envision their American Dream retirement is the opportunity to give back—to make contributions to people and causes they value. If, as we're working on your particular retirement puzzle together, we discover that this is one of your priorities, we'll plan for it. We'll also agree to limits—guardrails, if you will—on the type and amount of contributions you can make while maintaining your own American Dream retirement.

For instance, if a couple wants to give money annually to their adult offspring or contribute to their church, we want to establish a budget for these gifts up front and make it part of the game plan. It could be that, say, $10,000 per year for all contributions to family and church is perfectly within a given couple's guardrails, but if they're tempted to give more, the train might jump the track (so to speak).

I once had a client who drove over his guardrails in just this manner. Recall Earl's story from chapter 4. Earl had a solid retirement game plan, and it included some discretionary money he could give away if he chose. Every month, Earl dropped by and directed us to give him a $10,000 draw from his nest egg. It was his money, and he could do what he chose with it, but contributing large sums of money to his daughter was shaking him away from his retirement plan.

As you might recall, Earl's daughter lived in a nice house worth more than a half million dollars. She drove a new vehicle and could certainly have had employment that paid her far more than she was making, but she didn't need to get a better job or cut back on her spending because her dad was giving her quite a bit of money every month. Her dad had already underwritten her college education and her time in the Peace Corps. He was even paying for her cell phone service and fitness club membership. You could say Earl was supporting his daughter's comfortable lifestyle while crumbling his own.

You can probably guess what happened next. Despite my best advice against his decision to blow through his nest egg in this way, Earl ran out of money.

I have great empathy for a person like Earl, who basically shook his own unshakeable retirement because he couldn't say no to his child. He's far from the only client I've had over the years who's been tempted to get off track. Most overcome that temptation with some solid advice from their retirement coach. Some, like Earl, don't.

In order to enjoy the unshakeable retirement you can have with a solid retirement game plan, you have to stick to your plan. Helping clients create a great game plan for their American Dream retirement is extremely rewarding, but in many cases it's only half the battle. Helping them stay on track is sometimes more difficult, but it can also be a deeply fulfilling part of the job. The key is reminding retired clients that they absolutely must balance the needs of those to whom they would like to give money with their own needs.

"Sam" and "Denise" had a son, Junior, who asked them for a large amount of money—more than their guardrails would call for—in order to start a business. It could be argued that Junior's entrepreneurial plan wasn't extremely solid, given the type of business he wanted to start. From Junior's perspective, he saw his mom and dad take off for nice overseas vacations twice a year, and he figured they could certainly afford to fund his start-up.

It's always hard to say no to someone you love, especially your son or daughter, but Sam and Denise found it in them to do it. "Junior," they said, "we're happy to give you some of the money you want, but we're on a fixed income, and the money we have has to last us the rest of our lives. We put off a lot of our dreams for these golden years of our retirement, and to be honest, our semiannual vacations are important to us.

We worked hard for many years to earn those vacations. We wish you luck with your venture, and God willing, some day you'll be able to say you worked hard and earned a few vacations for yourself."

Balance. It's critical. Sure, you want to help your kids and your church and other causes you feel strongly about, but you have to balance those contributions within the guardrails of your American Dream retirement game plan.

In my experience, the people who are making poor money choices are usually the ones who really can't afford it. Meanwhile, those who could afford to help out their offspring typically are the ones who have raised their kids to stand on their own two feet and don't need to worry about supporting them later in their adult lives.

The Most Important Guardrails

We've discussed some of the important guardrails your game plan will need to succeed. There are three more that I would call the most important guardrails.

The first is an emergency fund. Your plan will certainly call for maintaining an emergency fund equivalent to six to twelve months of your expenses. When you need expensive home or auto repairs, you'll have the money in your emergency fund to cover that expense. Or when a family member needs emergency assistance due to a medical or employment problem that arises, you can help in that area as well. As long as you gradually replenish your emergency fund, it's there when you need it. The amount of money in that fund is a limit—a guardrail—on what you can afford to do to help out in an emergency.

The second guardrail is to get and stay out of debt. We covered this in the previous chapter, but debt is one of the biggest opponents to your American Dream retirement. If you can get out of debt, the next step is to avoid the temptation to take on new debt when you no longer have the regular paychecks you would need to repay it. If you establish a hard-and-fast rule that you won't get into any new debt, you'll have given yourself another valuable guardrail.

The third guardrail is a properly balanced portfolio. Your plan will call for a nice balance of money in each of the three investment worlds. You'll have cash (particularly in your emergency fund), you'll have some money invested in high-growth instruments such as stocks, and you'll have a large share of your nest egg in that middle world of linked accounts that guarantee you won't lose your principal but that you'll have income coming in to pay all your bills and do the fun stuff you always wanted to do. As long as you're not playing too heavily in the go-for-broke investment world of high growth and high risk—as long as your funds there are limited—you have another important guardrail.

You don't want to keep the lion's share of your nest egg in the stock market and hope to live off that fund. As we've described earlier, that's a path for a train wreck disaster to your American Dream retirement.

At this point, your focus needs to be on preservation of your nest egg and your income and not on going for big growth numbers.

We all know what happens when you're trying to live off your principal by taking a draw of, say, 5 percent each year on a million-dollar stock account. Once the market experiences a big correction—for example, 30 percent—your million-dollar account now holds only $700,000. In order to maintain your $50,000 annual draws, you would have to deplete your principal by something like 7 percent each year. Do the math. This is a train that could easily jump the track. You could run out of money, even without funding a son or daughter's comfortable lifestyle the way Earl did.

Stick to Your American Dream

I've referred to a few sports movies in *Unshakeable Retirement*, but I saved my favorite for last. *Field of Dreams* is a movie full of characters who hold onto their dreams, sometimes against seemingly overwhelming odds.

Kevin Costner portrays the main character in the movie, a man who's struggling to make ends meet as a corn farmer in Iowa. A "voice" awakens him in the middle of the night, telling him, "If you build it, he will come."[4] He continues to hear the voice throughout the movie, and he becomes convinced that he needs to build a baseball field so that a long-dead star player can come back and play ball there. Despite a great

---

4   Alden Robinson, Phil. 1989. *Field of Dreams.* Gordon Company.

deal of pushback from everyone, from his wife to the other farmers in town, Costner's character plows under a large portion of his corn crop and builds a stunning baseball field.

James Earl Jones has another major role in the film. He's the retired author of a protest-culture book from the 1960s. Despite his own desire to be left alone, he ends up accompanying Costner's character to a baseball game, where he too hears the voice. The two men see a reference on the stadium scoreboard to a long-gone ball player, and they decide to travel to Minnesota to find out why this player only played in the major leagues for one half inning, many years earlier, without ever having a chance at bat.

In the small Minnesota town, one that would be very familiar to my family, Costner's character meets the town doctor, played by Burt Lancaster. It's a miraculous chance meeting. Costner's character finds himself on the streets of town at night and is shocked to learn he's been transported back in time to the early 1970s, when the doctor was nearing his death after a long career of service as the town's physician. Costner asks him why he didn't stay with baseball. "Most men would consider it a tragedy," he says, to come so close to their dream without realizing it.

"If I'd only been a doctor for fifteen minutes," Lancaster's character says, "that would have been a tragedy."[5]

---

5   Alden Robinson, Phil. 1989. *Field of Dreams.* Gordon Company.

Later, Jones and Costner pick up a hitchhiker, and it turns out to be the younger version of Lancaster's character, on his way to try his luck as a baseball player. All three of the men end up on the "Field of Dreams" in Iowa, where many dreams are fulfilled near the end of the movie.

Lancaster's younger-version character gets to hit the ball, but then he steps off the field and is transformed back into the elderly doctor, where he saves Costner's daughter from choking to death on a hot dog. He walks off into the cornfield to join the other players, who had been walking onto the field from deep in the corn to play ball but then disappearing each night back into the corn. Lancaster's character gets to join them in "heaven," where his multiple dreams are fulfilled. James Earl Jones' character is also invited into the corn, where he'll be able to fulfill his own long-held dream to write about baseball—a dream he had kept secret for decades.

Costner's character is not invited into the corn. He has to stay in Iowa. As the rest of the players are leaving, one (the catcher) stays after the game. It turns out to be Costner's father, from whom he had been estranged since before his dad's death. As the father fulfills his own dream of being able to play major league baseball on the Field of Dreams, Costner's character gets to fulfill his deep-seated dream by having a chance to play catch with his dad and reconcile with him as the young man he never knew.

All three characters saw their dreams become reality,

in spite of opposition from those around them and in spite of the difficult circumstances in their "real" lives that mirror the tough things that happen to all of us. Did they have guardrails? Not in all cases. The most important guardrails were the ones inside them—the passionate dedication to their dreams that no opponent could derail.

In the case of this wonderful fantasy tale, for some of the characters, not even death could part them from their American Dreams. They all did help others, but in a way that didn't cause them to derail themselves. They were there, with just the help that was needed, at just the time it was needed, and they still went on to fulfill their own dreams.

They were unshakeable.

* * *

You worked hard your whole career, and you earned the right to have your unshakeable American Dream retirement. You got professional, expert help from your retirement coach, and you ended up with a game plan that assured you could have that unshakeable retirement—as long as you stick to the plan.

Generosity is a virtue. Helping and contributing are fantastic instincts to have and great habits to develop. Nevertheless, don't get shaken out of your own American Dream retirement. Be kind but disciplined. After all, it's great to be in a position to help someone you love when the need arises, but you also want to be in a position to help the next time assistance is truly needed.

Stay inside your guardrails. Keep the train on the track. You'll thank yourself, and you'll also have the gratitude of those you've been able to help as a result of your disciplined, unshakeable generosity. You'll also be assured of living the American Dream retirement you worked so hard to earn.

CONCLUSION

Welcome to the finish line, the end zone, the winner's circle, the checkered flag!

I love seeing the pure joy on the faces of players in a champion team's locker room after they've won the Super Bowl, the World Series, the Stanley Cup, or the NBA Finals. Champagne flows, laughter rings out, and there's a smile on every face. Like my high school football team, they worked hard, created and stuck to an ingenious game plan, and also had a little luck. (I'll quickly point out that we didn't have champagne in our locker room after we won the state championship, nor at any other time. We were kids, after all.)

In chapter 1, I asked you to envision what a true American Dream retirement would be for you, specifically, given your priorities for your golden years. After reading *Unshakeable Retirement,* I hope you see that this dream is not just an aspiration—it has every chance of being a reality. It may seem a little terrifying at first. But oh, the exhilaration, when we see the plan come together!

Dale (bottom left) celebrates with his team after the championship game.

Just come on in, dump the puzzle pieces onto the table, and let's start solving it together. Let's look at how we can use the right balance of the three investment worlds, and some discipline, to make sure you have the money you need to fund your American Dream retirement. Let's explore ways to make sure you're living the way you want to live in your go-go, slow-go, and no-go years, with everything taken care of so that you don't have to worry about money. Let's also see if we can still have something left to leave to the ones you care about most.

I was tickled when a client couple recently told me they were off to their SKI club.

"Ski club?" I asked, taking the bait. "Are you, uh, active skiers these days?"

This was a couple in their seventies and still very much in their go-go years—but skiing? I just couldn't picture that for them.

"Not downhill skiing," they said. "The SKI club. S. K. I. Spending the Kids' Inheritance."

It was their way of saying they were off to another pleasant vacation and enjoying their lives rather than hoarding their money, only to leave it to their kids to go on nice vacations, join country clubs, or do any of the other fun things they had envisioned for their own American Dream retirement. I'm sure they'll still have a nice inheritance to leave their kids. They just won't deprive themselves of the fun golden years they worked so hard to earn.

* * *

Now that you know what kind of winning game plan you can put together with hard work, ingenuity, courage, and a little luck, it's time to revisit your vision from chapter 1: What kind of retirement would be perfect for you? What's your American Dream?

Find a great coach, create a winning plan, and stick to it. You can have that American Dream retirement. If I can be of assistance, please don't hesitate to reach out. I can't wait to celebrate with you—with or without the champagne.

DALE L. TONDRYK
Tondryk Wealth Management, LLC
www.myinvestingcoach.com
dale@tondrykfinancial.com
(952) 401-1671

ABOUT THE AUTHOR

DALE L. TONDRYK is the president and founder of Tondryk Wealth Management, LLC, a registered investment advisory firm headquartered in Minnetonka, Minnesota. Dale brings more than thirty years' financial experience to work for his firm's clients, and he has offered his expertise to thousands of investors through seminars on financial planning, retirement strategies, and wealth transfer.

Minnesota listeners will recall Dale's popular radio program, *The Retirement Playbook*, and he now offers regularly scheduled podcasts for a growing audience of fans. He also coauthored a book by the same title.

Dale Tondryk grew up in a small town in northern Minnesota, where he learned the importance of family, leadership, and commitment. These are the values that have formed the bedrock of Dale's career and are at the core of his successful philosophy in helping clients discover (and successfully apply) the key principles of investing and wealth creation that help fuel their American Dreams.

Dale's passion is to help lead people to financial freedom. His clients attest to his unique ability to explain things simply and to inspire them to lives of wealth preservation and balance. His focus on the most important aspects of his clients' financial lives helps them achieve strong peace of mind through greater portfolio diversification, lower overall risk, and increased expected rate of return. Dale is committed to educating and empowering individuals toward active participation in their own financial futures.

As part of his mission, Dale is a dedicated member of the National Ethics Association (Ethics.net).

Dale and his wife, Katherine, enjoy spending time with their children and grandchildren, as well as with members of their extended family in Duluth and Brainerd. Their active lifestyle includes golfing, hiking, biking, and traveling.